WILD WEST TRIVIA

THE WILD WEST TRIVIA SERIES:

COWBOY
TRIVIA

BY RICK STEBER

WILD WEST TRIVIA

Copyright © 2017
by Rick Steber

All rights reserved. No part of the material protected by this copyright notice may be reproduced or utilized in any form or by any means, electronic or mechanical, including photocopying, recording or by any informational storage and retrieval system without written permission from the copyright owner.

ISBN: 978-0-945134-47-3

Printed and bound in the United States of America by
Maverick Publications • Bend, Oregon

 COWBOY

THE WILD WEST TRIVIA SERIES:

Cowboy Trivia is one book from the Wild West Trivia series. Each book is designed to challenge a reader's knowledge and expertise relating to American history, the great outdoors and the wide panorama of the Western landscape. This series is educational and a fun way for children, friends and families to learn. Oftentimes a question or answer will serve as a springboard into other discussions, remembrances or related stories.

Turn *Cowboy Trivia* into an entertaining game by having one person read a question aloud. The opponent, or team of players, selects an answer.

The reader turns the page and reads aloud the correct answer. This is a wonderful way to pass the miles while traveling, or as rousing entertainment around a crackling campfire. Have fun while you learn, and keep score if you wish. Collect the entire series.

 **COWBOY**

QUESTION

If a cowboy was to *mosey*, at what pace would he be traveling?

- A. Brisk
- B. Leisurely
- C. Creeping

ANSWER ON NEXT PAGE

ANSWER

If a cowboy was to mosey, he would move along at a leisurely pace and be in no particular sort of hurry.

QUESTION

What is an *Appaloosa*?

    A. Breed of cow dogs
    B. Type of rope
    C. Spotted horse

ANSWER ON
NEXT PAGE

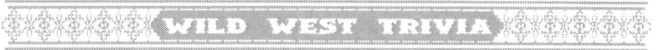

ANSWER

Appaloosa is a breed of horses developed by the Nez Perce Indians of the Northwest. The horses are characterized by colored spots on their rumps, pink on their noses and white in their eyes.

QUESTION

What does it mean to *see daylight*?

- A. Riding rough
- B. Sun has come up
- C. Better times are on the horizon

ANSWER ON
NEXT PAGE

ANSWER

It is not good when rodeo spectators see daylight because it means a cowboy is leaving the saddle on every jump and daylight can be seen between him and the bronc. In such a situation it is normally only a matter of time before the cowboy gets thrown about as far as a desert buzzard can smell an open canteen.

QUESTION

What are *batwings*?

- A. Chaps
- B. Bar drink
- C. Wings of a bat

ANSWER ON
NEXT PAGE

ANSWER

Batwings are chaps made of heavy bull hide. They have wing-like attachments over the legs and are popular because they can easily be snapped on, unlike shotgun chaps which require the wearer to remove his spurs before pulling on, or shedding, his chaps.

QUESTION

What does *bedding down* mean?

- A. Making a bed
- B. Planting a garden
- C. Putting cows to sleep

ANSWER ON
NEXT PAGE

ANSWER

This term was used during the cattle drive era. At the end of the day the cowboys would work the cattle onto an open, level section of ground where they would be bedded down for the night. Some of the cattle would remain standing but others would lie down and contentedly chew their cuds.

COWBOY

QUESTION

What is a *bedroll*?

- A. Where a cowboy sleeps
- B. Pocket change
- C. A game played around campfires

ANSWER ON NEXT PAGE

ANSWER

Next to a good horse and a saddle, a cowboy's most valued possession is his bedroll. A bedroll consists of a canvas tarpaulin and blankets or quilts and is designed to keep a man warm and dry.

QUESTION

If a cowboy talks about his *John B*, what is he talking about?

- A. Saddle
- B. Hat
- C. Boots

ANSWER ON NEXT PAGE

ANSWER

A cowboy takes pride in his Stetson hat, named after its maker John B. Stetson. It takes years to wear out a Stetson. Over time a cowboy hat can pick up a lot of trail dust and more than a few odd smells. Some hats have been known to smell worse than hell on house-cleaning day.

QUESTION

What does the term *belly-up* mean?

- A. A bad bucking horse
- B. Protruding stomach, the result of drinking too much beer
- C. Standing at a bar

ANSWER ON NEXT PAGE

ANSWER

A cowboy will occasionally belly-up to the bar for a drink. One cowboy who could not seem to handle his liquor said, "Ain't no use for me to belly-up to the bar 'cause alcohol and me mix together about as harmoniously as a deaf man banging on a harp with a sledge hammer."

QUESTION

Name the river known as the *Big Muddy*.

    A. Mississippi
    B. Colorado
    C. Missouri

ANSWER ON
NEXT PAGE

ANSWER

When a cowboy talks about the Big Muddy he most often is referring to the Missouri River. According to one old hand, "Anythin' east of the Big Muddy don't amount ta a hill a beans."

COWBOY

QUESTION

When a cowboy talks about a *bit*, what does he mean?

    A. Small amount of most anything
    B. Pinch of tobacco
    C. Metal bar that goes in a horse's mouth

ANSWER ON NEXT PAGE

ANSWER

There are many types of bits that go in a horse's mouth and are used to control the horse. An experienced cowboy riding a well-trained horse does not need a bit for control and many cowboys ride with nothing more than a hackamore—a halter with reins.

QUESTION

When a cowboy talks about a *blaze* what is he most likely referring to?

   A. Range fire
   B. Identifying feature on a horse
   C. Mark cut into a tree

ANSWER ON
NEXT PAGE

ANSWER

A cowboy will notice all identifying features on a horse, especially a blaze, a light-colored mark on a horse generally extending from near the eyes to the nose.

 **COWBOY**

QUESTION

What is a *blizzard*?

- A. Ice cream treat
- B. Snow storm
- C. A scavenger bird

ANSWER ON
NEXT PAGE

ANSWER

A blizzard is a storm that comes with a cold north wind and sleet or snow. Sometimes it will be too cold riding into a blizzard and a cowboy will have to drift with the wind. By the time the storm finally blows itself out the cowboy will find himself miles away from his home ranch.

QUESTION

What is a *bone yard*?

   A. Cemetery
   B. Jell-O factory
   C. Scene of a gun fight

ANSWER ON
NEXT PAGE

ANSWER

The cowboy's name for a cemetery is bone yard. A bone yard is also the place, usually a dry wash or a spot away from the ranch house, where dead animals are left for the birds, wild animals and insects to pick the bones clean.

QUESTION

What is *buck fever*?

- A. Sickness brought on by eating venison
- B. A case of nerves
- C. Greed

ANSWER ON NEXT PAGE

ANSWER

Buck fever is a rare nervous condition that can occasionally strike even the most experienced hunter and is usually caused by the sight of an exceptionally large buck. Hunters stricken with buck fever have been known to allow a deer to run past them without ever firing a shot.

QUESTION

If a cowboy gets *buffaloed,* what has happened to him?

   A. Trampled
   B. Bowled over
   C. Mentally confused

ANSWER ON
NEXT PAGE

ANSWER

A man who gets buffaloed is most often mentally confused over something that has happened and has not quite figured out what has befallen him. One time a cowboy playing cards claimed, "When that fellar laid down his flush beating my straight I was about as buffaloed as a blind bear in a briar patch."

QUESTION

What is a *desert canary*?

- A. Meadow lark
- B. Mule
- C. Gold finch

ANSWER ON
NEXT PAGE

ANSWER

A mule, because of its loud braying, is sometimes referred to as a desert canary. A cowboy once claimed, "I won't have nothin' ta do with a mule. They're as full of venom as a rattlesnake in the middle of August."

QUESTION

What does *mugging* a steer involve?

    A. Pushing over a sleeping steer
    B. Jumping on a steer and throwing it to the ground
    C. Drinking from a steer's horn

ANSWER ON NEXT PAGE

ANSWER

In rodeo, the man who mugs a steer drops from the saddle of a running horse and wrestles a steer to the ground. Bill Pickett, an African-American cowboy performed the stunt as a rodeo exhibition in 1910. He kept the critter on the ground for several minutes by biting its nose.

COWBOY

QUESTION

Name the one thing a bull rope must have.

- A. Pink ribbon
- B. Bell
- C. Noose

ANSWER ON
NEXT PAGE

ANSWER

There are no knots or hitches in a bull rope. The bull rider fastens the loose rope around the bull in such a manner that it will come free when the rider opens his hand at the end of the ride. Fastened to the rope is a bell that hangs under the bull's belly.

 COWBOY

QUESTION

If a cowboy has a *caboodle* exactly what does he have?

   A. Everything
   B. Nothing
   C. Bull calf

ANSWER ON
NEXT PAGE

ANSWER

A caboodle is cowboy lingo for the whole amount, everything, nothing held back. Sometimes the saying is expanded to "the whole kit and caboodle".

QUESTION

What are *calf fries*?

- A. Same as Rocky Mountain oysters
- B. Scalloped potatoes
- C. Fried veal

ANSWER ON
NEXT PAGE

ANSWER

Calf fries and Rocky Mountain oysters are the same thing, the fried testicles from castrated bull calves. They are considered a delicacy.

QUESTION

If a cowboy gets a case of *calico fever,* what sort of ailment has stricken him?

    A. Having to wash laundry
    B. Lovesickness
    C. Allergy to cotton cloth

ANSWER ON
NEXT PAGE

ANSWER

In the old days a cowboy would refer to a woman as a calico because that was the dress material women commonly wore. When a man was struck with a case of calico fever it meant he was lovesick.

QUESTION

What is *bareback riding*?

    A. Riding without a saddle
    B. Riding without a shirt
    C. Riding naked

ANSWER ON
NEXT PAGE

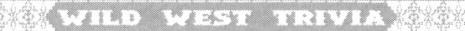

ANSWER

Bareback riding is one of the five standard rodeo events. The rider has no saddle, stirrups, bridle or rein. Instead, the rider grips a bareback rigging, a leather handhold cinched on a horse, and tries to hold on while spurring the horse for 8 seconds.

 COWBOY

QUESTION

In cowboy lingo what is a *cartwheel*?

- A. Wheel on a pony cart
- B. Somersault performed by rodeo cheerleaders
- C. Silver dollar

ANSWER ON
NEXT PAGE

ANSWER

Cowboys sometimes called silver dollars cartwheels because of the way a silver dollar twirled and flipped when tossed in the air.

 COWBOY

QUESTION

If a cowboy is staying in the *calaboose*, where is he spending his time?

    A. The last car of a train
    B. Saloon
    C. Jail

ANSWER ON
NEXT PAGE

ANSWER

Calaboose comes from the Spanish word calabozo, which means jail. A cowboy who finds himself in such a predicament is about as happy at his prospects as a woodpecker in a petrified forest.

QUESTION

What is typically used to *rim-fire* a horse?

- A. Extra measure of grain
- B. Alfalfa hay
- C. A burr

ANSWER ON
NEXT PAGE

ANSWER

All it takes to rim-fire a horse is to place a burr under the saddle blanket and wait until the rider climbs aboard. The horse will do everything in its power to buck away the irritation. This is a prank cowboys play on one another strictly for amusement.

QUESTION

What is a *saddle-blanket gambler*?

- A. Man who gambles for saddle blankets
- B. Man who bets he can ride a particular horse
- C. Small-time gambler

ANSWER ON
NEXT PAGE

ANSWER

A saddle-blanket gambler travels the range and gambles with the cowboys, spreading his saddle blanket on the ground as the table. Charlie Russell, the famous western painter, said, "You can tell a lot about a saddle-blanket gambler's luck by takin' a close look at the horse an' riggin' he rode in on."

 **COWBOY**

QUESTION

In the old days if a cowboy was *carvin' scallops* what would he be doing?

    A. Eating a seafood dinner
    B. Castrating a bull calf
    C. Notching his shooting iron

ANSWER ON
NEXT PAGE

ANSWER

A cowboy who was carvin' scallops would be a gunfighter giving himself credit for killing a man by cutting a notch on the grip of his shooting iron. A gunfighter once bragged, "I could draw and fire my six-gun quicker than a normal fellar could spit and holler howdy."

COWBOY

QUESTION

What is a *dry camp*?

   A. Camp without alcohol
   B. Camp without rain
   C. Camp without water

ANSWER ON
NEXT PAGE

ANSWER

A dry camp is a camp set miles from the nearest water. A cowboy once claimed, "We was dry-camped so far out in the pucker brush, why I had ta prime myself 'fore I could muster a spit."

QUESTION

What is a *casa grande*?

- A. Ranch house
- B. Mexican food
- C. Large casa

ANSWER ON
NEXT PAGE

ANSWER

Cowboys in the Southwest use the Spanish casa grande to denote the home ranch of a large spread or when talking about the ranch owner's home.

 **COWBOY**

QUESTION

If an old ranch hand was about to *cash in his chips* what would he be doing?

- A. Buying into a poker game
- B. Getting ready to die
- C. Starting a fire with buffalo chips

ANSWER ON
NEXT PAGE

ANSWER

If an old buckaroo claimed, "I got half a mind just ta cash in my chips," it meant he was thinking about dying.

QUESTION

Who was *Cattle Kate*?

- A. Cattle rustler
- B. Dance hall queen
- C. Famous singer

ANSWER ON
NEXT PAGE

ANSWER

Ella Waterson, better known as Cattle Kate, was accused of stealing cattle during the Wyoming Rustler's War in 1889. She was hanged alongside her companion, Jim Averill. The name Cattle Kate is applied to any woman suspected of taking another man's cattle.

QUESTION

What is a *cattle lick*?

   A. The way cattle naturally clean themselves
   B. A bug that can infect cattle
   C. Geographic feature that attracts cattle

ANSWER ON
NEXT PAGE

ANSWER

A cattle lick is a naturally occurring geographic feature where salt is present in the soil. Cattle come here to lick for the salt. A cattle lick is also the location where salt and mineral blocks are placed by cowboys and where cattle gather to lick the blocks.

 COWBOY

QUESTION

What does it mean if a cowboy gets *caught in his own loop*?

    A. He is throwing too big a loop
    B. He has failed
    C. His rope has a kink in it

ANSWER ON
NEXT PAGE

ANSWER

If a cowboy gets caught in his own loop it means that he has failed at something and that it was his own fault. In such a case he has no one to blame but himself and more than likely he will simply shake his head and mutter something like, "All I know about brains is ya can't buy 'em scrambled."

QUESTION

What is a *cavvy*?

- A. A remuda
- B. A group of calves
- C. Anything that acts like a young calf

ANSWER ON
NEXT PAGE

ANSWER

Cavvy comes from the Spanish word caballada and is interchangeable with remuda. Cavvy and remuda are terms for the extra mounts a cowboy keeps for riding. Most working cowboys keep 8 to 10 horses in their cavvy and alternate using them so every horse is fresh and ready to give a full day's work.

 **COWBOY**

QUESTION

If a cowboy was *choking the horn* what would he be doing?

    A. Driving an automobile in heavy traffic
    B. Blowing air through a cow horn
    C. Gripping the saddle horn

ANSWER ON NEXT PAGE

ANSWER

If a horse gets to acting as crazy as popcorn in a hot skillet it might cause a cowboy to grab the saddle horn. Such an action would require his friends to tease him about choking the horn.

 COWBOY

QUESTION

If a cowboy was *caught short* what happened?

- A. Unarmed
- B. Short in stature
- C. Tried to escape but was quickly captured

ANSWER ON NEXT PAGE

ANSWER

If a cowboy was caught short it meant he found himself unarmed in a moment of crisis. A cowboy once said, "You don't wanna be caught short, especially when you're close enough ta hell ta smell the smoke."

 COWBOY

QUESTION

What does the term *chute* mean to a working cowboy?

    A. A saying similar to "dog-gone-it"
    B. If a cowboy gets bucked real high he needs a "chute" to come down
    C. A narrow passageway

ANSWER ON NEXT PAGE

ANSWER

A chute is a narrow-fenced lane through which cattle are run. It is also an enclosure from which riders, mounted on either horses or bulls, are released into a rodeo arena.

QUESTION

What is a *circle horse*?

- A. Roundup horse
- B. Trick horse
- C. Rodeo horse trained to run barrels

ANSWER ON
NEXT PAGE

ANSWER

A circle horse is used during roundup and is part of a cowboy's cavvy. These horses are especially hearty, have a great deal of endurance and are proficient at cutting cows and calves from the herd. A cowboy once claimed, "My circle horse is so good at cutting he can separate out fly specks from a can of pepper."

QUESTION

What does the term *backfire* mean to a cowboy on the range?

    A. Ailment caused by consuming too many beans
    B. Out-of-time automobile
    C. Attempt to counter a wildfire

ANSWER ON NEXT PAGE

ANSWER

A backfire is a fire purposely set to counter a range fire. The backfire will burn away the combustible material and when the wildfire reaches the burned over area it will burn itself out.

QUESTION

What does the expression *come undone* mean to a cowboy?

- A. His fly is open
- B. Something has gone wrong
- C. A horse has commenced bucking

ANSWER ON
NEXT PAGE

ANSWER

Come undone means that a horse has commenced bucking in an aggressive manner and all the cowboy can do is stick as tight as a tick in a lamb's tail and hope the horse bucks himself out in a hurry.

 **COWBOY**

QUESTION

If a cowboy *takes a dally* what is he doing?

- A. Wasting the afternoon
- B. Spending time with a gal
- C. Taking a half-hitch around the saddle horn with a rope

ANSWER ON
NEXT PAGE

ANSWER

If a cowboy takes a dally he is roping calves and has thrown a loop, made the catch and is in the process of tying a half-hitch around the saddle horn. The loose end of the rope is held in the roper's hand so he can let it slip or shorten it, depending on what the calf does.

COWBOY

QUESTION

What is a *cookie*?

    A. Camp cook
    B. Dessert
    C. A circle maneuver performed horseback

ANSWER ON
NEXT PAGE

ANSWER

Cookie is the affectionate name cowboys often give to the range cook. It is Cookie who prepares three hot meals a day and, if the cowboys treat him right, the food is good and there is sufficient quantity to keep everyone as happy as a puppy that has two tails to chase.

QUESTION

What is a *belly wash*?

- A. Weak coffee
- B. Shower
- C. Sudden rainstorm

ANSWER ON NEXT PAGE

ANSWER

A cowboy refers to weak coffee as belly wash. A cowboy wants his coffee strong enough to float a horse shoe. One cowboy claimed, "Without a stiff jolt of caffeine I'm liable to act as puny as a frozen rattlesnake."

QUESTION

What does it mean if a cowboy is swinging a *big loop*?

- A. Catching a difficult calf
- B. Champion roper
- C. Cattle thief

ANSWER ON NEXT PAGE

ANSWER

A cowboy who swings a big loop is most often procuring stock that belongs to another man. A rancher once said, "I ain't out-'n-out sayin' he's a cattle rustler, but mind ya he does throw himself a mighty big loop".

QUESTION

If a cowboy is *coyotin' 'round* what is he doing?

    A. Sneaking around
    B. Howling about an injustice
    C. Baying at the moon

ANSWER ON
NEXT PAGE

ANSWER

A cowboy who is coyotin' 'round is being sneaky or hiding out because he is in trouble with either the law or a woman.

QUESTION

What does *crow hop* mean?

A. The way crows hop when grain is spilled on the ground
B. Jumping a freight train
C. Antics of a horse

ANSWER ON NEXT PAGE

ANSWER

A horse will sometimes crow hop or make a pretense at bucking by arching its back and leaping stiff-kneed in the air. This is not intended to unseat a rider but merely to let the rider know that the horse has a bit of extra spirit or is mildly upset at having to go to work.

 **COWBOY**

QUESTION

If a cowboy is stricken with *cupid's cramp* what sort of ailment is he suffering?

    A. Groin pull
    B. Lovesick
    C. Too old to cut the mustard

ANSWER ON
NEXT PAGE

ANSWER

If a cowboy comes down with a serious case of cupid's cramp it means he has fallen in love. There is an old cowboy saying that goes: "Only two things will turn a cowboy's head, a good-looking horse and a good-looking woman. Both will make him whistle. Proving only one thing, he's still young enough to pucker."

QUESTION

What does it mean if a cowboy is about to *cut his suspenders*?

    A. Drop his pants
    B. Leave the ranch
    C. Get divorced

ANSWER ON
NEXT PAGE

WILD WEST TRIVIA

ANSWER

If a cowboy is about to cut his suspenders it means he is quitting the ranch where he has been working and is moving on to a new location and a change in scenery.

 **COWBOY**

QUESTION

What is a *cutting horse*?

- A. Horse trained to separate cattle
- B. Horse that has the habit of running into barbwire
- C. A gelding

ANSWER ON
NEXT PAGE

ANSWER

A good cutting horse is a cowboy's most valuable possession. It is specially trained to cut a particular cow from the herd and keep her separated. Such a horse embodies a combination of confidence, courage, intelligence, agility, speed and anticipation. A cowboy is lucky if he owns one such horse in a lifetime.

COWBOY

QUESTION

What does it mean if a cowboy *takes a cow to town*?

    A. Taking an unattractive girl to the movie
    B. Hauling a cow to the sale
    C. Pushing a cow to a new pasture

ANSWER ON NEXT PAGE

ANSWER

When a cowboy takes a cow to town it means that particular cow has been culled from the herd for a variety of reasons and she is being taken to the auction sale.

COWBOY

QUESTION

What is an *arroyo*?

    A. Cut-bank
    B. Kid's toy
    C. Sticky mud

ANSWER ON
NEXT PAGE

ANSWER

Arroyo comes from the Spanish word meaning "small creek". In cowboy country the term usually refers to a place where a small creek has cut a wash into the earth, creating a narrow gorge with steep-sided walls.

 **COWBOY**

QUESTION

In rodeo terms what does *best average* mean?

    A. Middle-of-the-road
    B. Top dog
    C. Mediocre

ANSWER ON NEXT PAGE

ANSWER

Each day's rodeo competition is referred to as a go-round and the top contestants are paid off in prize money for the best ride, or time, in each event. The one who wins the most cumulative money in his chosen event during the rodeo wins the best average.

QUESTION

What has happened if a man *belly-ups, bucks out, cashes in, hangs up his spurs* or *has gone on his last roundup*?

- A. Quit the life of a cowboy
- B. Got married
- C. Dropped dead

ANSWER ON NEXT PAGE

ANSWER

If a man belly-ups, bucks out, cashes in, hangs up his spurs or goes on his last roundup, it is akin to shaking hands with Saint Peter or pushing up a field of daisies. It means he has died.

COWBOY

QUESTION

What is a *democrat wagon*?

- A. Light wagon
- B. Wagon that only goes to the left
- C. Wagon pulled by mules

ANSWER ON
NEXT PAGE

ANSWER

A democrat wagon is a light spring wagon used for hauling salt or fence wire but not for heavy hauling.

COWBOY

QUESTION

If a cowboy were to throw a *diamond hitch* what would he be doing?

    A. Packing
    B. Getting engaged
    C. Getting married

ANSWER ON
NEXT PAGE

ANSWER

If a cowboy were to throw a diamond hitch it would mean he was using a rope, interlaced on top in the figure of a diamond, to fasten a pack onto a horse or mule.

QUESTION

What is a *dogie*?

   A. Any cow dog
   B. Any calf
   C. Orphaned calf

ANSWER ON
NEXT PAGE

ANSWER

A dogie is not just any calf, as popularized by western writers and singers; to a working cowboy the name applies only to an undersized, motherless calf.

QUESTION

What is a cowboy doing if he is *cutting the dust, painting his tonsils, baying at the moon* or *seeing the elephant dance*?

   A. On a trail drive
   B. Drinking
   C. Riding night herd

ANSWER ON
NEXT PAGE

WILD WEST TRIVIA

ANSWER

If a man is cutting the dust, painting his tonsils, baying at the moon or seeing the elephant dance it is a sure-fire cinch he is in the drinking mood. By the time the sun comes up he will be lucky to hit the ground with his hat even if he gets three chances.

 **COWBOY**

QUESTION

What is a cowboy doing if he is *on the dodge*?

- A. Buying a new pickup truck
- B. Running from the law
- C. Leaving a woman who has marriage on her mind

ANSWER ON NEXT PAGE

ANSWER

A man who is on the dodge is generally trying to stay a jump or two ahead of the law. He may leave the country so fast he forgets to take his right name with him and makes so much dust in going that it will take a day or two for it to settle.

COWBOY

QUESTION

What does *elbow room* refer to?

- A. Wide-open spaces
- B. Enough room to drink at the bar
- C. Short-sleeve shirt

ANSWER ON
NEXT PAGE

ANSWER

In the old days if a homesteader took a claim anywhere on the range, even if it were 20 miles from the nearest neighbor, the newcomer would be paid a visit. The local rancher would complain that his elbow room and the wide-open spaces were being infringed upon by the newcomer.

QUESTION

If a cowboy is *sharpening his hoe, counting coup* or *locking horns,* what activity is he involved in?

- A. Fighting
- B. Dancing
- C. Riding broncs

ANSWER ON NEXT PAGE

ANSWER

If a man is sharpening his hoe, counting coup or locking horns he is involved in a fight or fixing to get into one. One cowboy commented about a fight he had been involved in, saying, "I was so skinned up my momma wouldn't have knowed me from a fresh-skinned hide."

QUESTION

Who is most likely to shout out *fire or fall back*?

    A. Cook
    B. Gunfighter
    C. Bartender

ANSWER ON
NEXT PAGE

ANSWER

When a cowboy dawdles too long filling his plate the cook is liable to shout, "Fire or fall back," which means the man should either hurry up and fill his plate or drop to the back of the food line.

QUESTION

When an old-time cowboy mentioned *fish* what was he referring to?

    A. Food
    B. Coat
    C. Boots

ANSWER ON
NEXT PAGE

ANSWER

The old-timers always rode with a yellow oilskin slicker tied behind the cantle of their saddles. It was called a fish because of the slicker's trademark logo. A man could go a year and never need his fish but the one day he was without it, he could count on it raining hard enough to drown a duck.

QUESTION

If a cowboy is *nimble-footed* what does that mean?

    A. Good dancer
    B. Fast on his feet
    C. Has a good horse under him

ANSWER ON
NEXT PAGE

ANSWER

A cowboy who is nimble-footed can move fast. A cowboy once commented about a friend, "Why he was as nimble-footed as a grasshopper in a pen of hungry chickens."

QUESTION

What is *burro milk*?

- A. Nonsense
- B. Any delicacy
- C. Whiskey

ANSWER ON NEXT PAGE

ANSWER

Burro milk is an old time cowboy expression for something absurd or for someone talking nonsense.

QUESTION

In the days of the cattle drives what did the term *following the tongue* mean?

    A. Following the boss's orders
    B. Reading the stars
    C. Watching the lead cow

ANSWER ON
NEXT PAGE

ANSWER

One method for the drovers to tell directions on a cattle drive was to read the stars. When the North Star was located, the wagon tongue was pointed in that direction. In the morning the drive started by simply following the tongue.

 COWBOY

QUESTION

What does it mean if a horse is *green-broke*?

- A. Ridden once or twice
- B. Only grazed on pasture grass
- C. Never fed hay or oats

ANSWER ON
NEXT PAGE

ANSWER

If a horse is only ridden a time or two, just enough to have the rough edges taken off, it is considered to be green-broke.

QUESTION

If a cowboy mentions *bait, bear sign, gun wading, wasp nest* and *splatter dab*, what is he talking about?

    A. Guns
    B. Grub
    C. Horses

ANSWER ON
NEXT PAGE

ANSWER

It was said that an outfit could keep a cowboy happy with good grub. Bait means a meal. Bear sign is doughnuts. Gun wading and wasp nests are light bread. And splatter dabs are hot cakes.

QUESTION

If a cowboy was *fryin' size* what did that mean?

    A. Fat
    B. Big
    C. Small

ANSWER ON
NEXT PAGE

ANSWER

If a cowboy was small in stature he would be termed frying size. Other terms cowboys used to describe a short cowboy was to say he was "sawed off at the pockets" or that he would have to "borrow a step-ladder to kick a grasshopper in the ankle".

 **COWBOY**

QUESTION

In what mood was a man if he was *all horns and rattles*?

    A. Talkative
    B. Angry
    C. Joking

ANSWER ON
NEXT PAGE

ANSWER

A cowboy once described a friend's sour mood by saying, "He was all horns and rattles, cantankerous as a buck in rut and dangerous as a cornered rattlesnake."

QUESTION

What is *gallin'*?

- A. About 4 quarts
- B. Courting
- C. A hat size

ANSWER ON
NEXT PAGE

ANSWER

If a cowboy courts a girl it is referred to as gallin'. According to one cowboy, "I went gallin' and was so lovestruck her old man poured cold water on the front porch steps just to keep me from sittin' there all night."

QUESTION

If a cowboy claims dinner is *nothin' but goat meat* what is it?

    A. Meat from a rustled steer
    B. Venison
    C. Goat meat

ANSWER ON NEXT PAGE

WILD WEST TRIVIA

ANSWER

A cowboy who is miles from civilization figures he has certain liberties coming to him. If the camp meat runs low he figures he has a constitutional right to kill a deer. Illegal venison is customarily referred to as goat meat.

QUESTION

What is a cowboy doing if he *bites the dust*?

- A. Bucking off a horse
- B. Taking a drink of alcohol
- C. Telling a windy

ANSWER ON
NEXT PAGE

ANSWER

When a cowboy bites the dust it means he is in the process of getting bucked off a horse. If he is lucky when he lands, he might have his hinges, bolts and nuts knocked loose but he won't have anything broken.

QUESTION

What does it mean if a cowboy, or a horse, is *on the goosey side*?

- A. Talkative
- B. Flighty
- C. Nervous

ANSWER ON
NEXT PAGE

ANSWER

If a man or a horse is goosey it means they are the nervous type and easily spooked. A cowboy once alluded to an acquaintance, saying, "He was 'bout as goosey as a long-tailed cat lying under a rocking chair."

QUESTION

What is a *go-round*?

- A. Rodeo competition
- B. Hitting every bar in town
- C. Roping every calf in the pen

ANSWER ON NEXT PAGE

ANSWER

In rodeo a "go-round" is complete when every contestant in an event has the opportunity to compete. In a small rodeo there may be a single go-round but in the National Finals Rodeo there are 10 go-rounds spread over a 10-day period.

QUESTION

What does the term *meat in the pot* refer to?

   A. Rifle
   B. Good hunter
   C. Call to dinner

ANSWER ON
NEXT PAGE

ANSWER

Out on the range a rifle is often referred to as meat in the pot because a good shooting rifle, in the hands of a skilled marksman, is almost a guarantee of having meat for dinner.

QUESTION

What type of a cowboy is a *greenhorn*?

- A. Experienced
- B. Inexperienced
- C. Rides for a single outfit

ANSWER ON
NEXT PAGE

WILD WEST TRIVIA

ANSWER

Cowboys call an inexperienced hand a greenhorn or a tenderfoot. One cowboy stated, "Why that fellar was such a greenhorn we had to ear him down and tie up a leg in order ta give 'em a haircut."

QUESTION

Why was *Boot Hill* famous?

- A. Cowboys left their old boots there
- B. It was a hill shaped like a boot
- C. Cemetery

ANSWER ON
NEXT PAGE

ANSWER

Boot Hill was a name given to many frontier cemeteries. Most of those who died in the lawless West were killed as a result of violence. They died with their boots on and most often were buried that way.

QUESTION

What is a *brand*?

- A. Trademark item
- B. Type of cereal
- C. Identifying mark on stock

ANSWER ON
NEXT PAGE

ANSWER

A brand is a registered mark that denotes ownership of an animal. In the days of the Old West a calf would be roped and dragged to the fire where a cowboy would burn the brand of the owner on the animal's hide. When the calf was turned loose on the open range the owner was easily recognized.

QUESTION

What happens if a rodeo cowboy *breaks the barrier*?

- A. 10 second penalty
- B. Exceeds the speed of sound
- C. Wins the event

ANSWER ON NEXT PAGE

WILD WEST TRIVIA

ANSWER

In a rodeo roping event, when the cowboy breaks the rope barrier before the calf or steer is clear of the chute area, the cowboy is assessed a penalty of an additional 10 seconds to his time.

QUESTION

What is the meaning of the word *cahoots*?

- A. Partnered-up
- B. Call of love-struck owls
- C. Crazy mustang

ANSWER ON
NEXT PAGE

ANSWER

If a cowboy goes into cahoots with another man it means he has thrown in with him, or become the man's partner.

 COWBOY

QUESTION

What does the cowboy term *bucket of blood* refer to?

    A. Unit of measure at a Red Cross blood drive
    B. Wild saloon
    C. A bad fight

ANSWER ON NEXT PAGE

ANSWER

Shorty Young owned a notorious saloon in Havre, Montana that was the original Bucket of Blood. Other unsavory frontier bars that lived up to the reputation of Shorty's place were often given the nickname, Bucket of Blood.

COWBOY

QUESTION

In the old days of the West who was the *guest of honor at a neck-tie party?*

    A. The groom at his wedding
    B. Preacher at a funeral
    C. A man being hanged

ANSWER ON
NEXT PAGE

ANSWER

A man who was caught rustling cattle or horses quickly became the guest of honor at a neck-tie party. A cowboy once said of a hanging he had attended, "It wasn't so much a case of stringin' up a fellar as it was simply a matter of a stiff neck happenin' ta meet the end of a short drop."

COWBOY

QUESTION

What is a *gully washer*?

    A. Violent rainstorm
    B. Free round of drinks
    C. Wildly funny tall tale

ANSWER ON
NEXT PAGE

ANSWER

When a sudden and violent storm hits the desert country the rain runs into, and washes down, the ravines and gullies. This can be a very dangerous situation and a cowboy caught in a gully-washer instinctively heads toward high ground.

 **COWBOY**

QUESTION

If a cowboy said he could not afford the *kitty* what would he be talking about?

    A. Card game
    B. Cat
    C. Barmaid

ANSWER ON
NEXT PAGE

ANSWER

There are times when a gambler's luck begins to run a little muddy. When he realizes all his money has been put into circulation and he can no longer afford to feed the card game kitty, he is finished until the next payday comes around.

QUESTION

What does the word *amigo* mean?

    A. Bandit
    B. Enemy
    C. Friend

ANSWER ON
NEXT PAGE

ANSWER

Amigo is a Spanish word which means a good friend, companion or a traveling buddy. It is said that if you consider another man an amigo you don't mind sharing a toothpick with him.

 COWBOY

QUESTION

What does the expression *leaving Cheyenne* mean?

    A. Leaving town and going back to the ranch
    B. A man giving up his cowboy way
    C. A man lighting out for parts unknown

ANSWER ON NEXT PAGE

ANSWER

The expression "leaving Cheyenne" means that a man is quitting where he is and heading out for somewhere new. The expression originated from the cowboy song, "Goodbye, Old Paint, I'm leavin' Cheyenne," which was usually played as the last song of the night at country dances.

COWBOY

QUESTION

If a cowboy is talking about *prairie dew, red-eye, bug juice* or *snake poison* what is he referring to?

    A. Medicine for cattle
    B. Alcohol
    C. Horse liniment

ANSWER ON
NEXT PAGE

ANSWER

Cowboys have a variety of colorful and descriptive names for alcoholic beverages.

QUESTION

If a cowboy is fixing his *makin's* what is he doing?

    A. Cooking bread
    B. Saddling his horse
    C. Rolling a smoke

ANSWER ON NEXT PAGE

ANSWER

A cowboy who is fixing his makin's is rolling a cigarette to smoke. The necessary materials include rolling paper and tobacco.

 **COWBOY**

QUESTION

Where is a cowboy if the shout goes out *man at the pot*!

    A. Around the campfire
    B. At the outhouse door
    C. At a branding

ANSWER ON
NEXT PAGE

ANSWER

According to camp etiquette, when a cowboy gets up to refill his cup from the coffee pot hanging over the campfire, if someone shouts, "Man at the pot!" the man at the coffee pot is required to fill everyone's cup.

QUESTION

How is news conveyed by the *moccasin telegraph*?

    A. Telephone
    B. Telegraph
    C. Grapevine

ANSWER ON
NEXT PAGE

ANSWER

News that travels over the moccasin telegraph is conveyed through the grapevine, one cowboy telling the next. It is always surprising how fast news can travel across the open range in this manner.

QUESTION

What is *muck-a-muck*?

    A. Spring thaw
    B. Adobe mud
    C. Grub

ANSWER ON
NEXT PAGE

ANSWER

Northwest cowboys sometimes call grub, or food, by the name muck-a-muck. This word is borrowed from the Cayuse Indian language.

QUESTION

What does the expression *ace high* come from?

    A. Poker
    B. Bar drink
    C. Bone in a horse's leg

ANSWER ON
NEXT PAGE

ANSWER

The term ace high comes from the game of poker and is a rather poor hand that includes no pairs of cards but features an ace as the highest card in the hand.

 COWBOY

QUESTION

What does the word *afoot* mean?

    A. Man without shoes
    B. Man without a horse
    C. One-legged man

ANSWER ON
NEXT PAGE

ANSWER

B

The old saying in cowboy country is that "a man on foot is no kind of man at all." A cowboy will do almost anything to keep a horse under him. So when a man is found afoot in cowboy country the assumption is he, or his horse, suffered some terrible accident.

QUESTION

Why would a cowboy put on *chaps*?

- A. Going to town and wanted to smell good
- B. Keep his lips soft
- C. Protect his legs

ANSWER ON
NEXT PAGE

ANSWER

Chaparreras is a Spanish word meaning leather breeches. The working cowboy shortened this to simply chaps. Chaps are worn to protect a rider's legs against brush, limbs, cacti, barbwire and as a shield against rain, snow and cold wind.

 **COWBOY**

QUESTION

What would a cowboy be doing if he was *cheeking*?

- A. Pulling a horse around
- B. Dancing with his favorite girl
- C. Sitting in a cold outhouse

ANSWER ON
NEXT PAGE

ANSWER

If a horse is unfamiliar to a cowboy he might cheek the horse as he mounts. In order to cheek a horse the cowboy grasps the bridle above the bit, pulls the horse's head toward him as he swings up onto the saddle. This maneuver pulls the horse off balance and gives the rider the advantage.

QUESTION

What is a *nice kitty*?

    A. Skunk
    B. Friendly barmaid
    C. Barn cat

ANSWER ON
NEXT PAGE

ANSWER

Sometimes a cowboy will refer to a skunk by the name nice kitty, which is really a misnomer because skunks are rarely nice.

WILD WEST TRIVIA

Wild West Trivia series was written and designed by award-winning author, Rick Steber. He has written more than forty books and has sold more than a million copies. For a complete listing of his books, or to see other titles in the Wild West Trivia series, visit www.ricksteber.com